at home with ...

The Ancient Greeks

...*in history*

WAYLAND

WAYLAND

This edition published in 2014 by Wayland

Copyright © 2014 Brown Bear Books Ltd.

Wayland
Hachette Children's Books
338 Euston Road
London NW1 3BH

Wayland Australia
Level 17/207 Kent Street
Sydney, NSW 2000

All Rights Reserved.

Brown Bear Books Ltd.
First Floor
9–17 St. Albans Place
London
N1 0NX

Author: Tim Cooke
Designer: Lynne Lennon
Picture manager: Sophie Mortimer
Design manager: Keith Davis
Editorial director: Lindsey Lowe
Children's publisher: Anne O'Daly

ISBN–13: 978 0 7502 8191 1

Printed in China

Wayland is a division of Hachette Children's Books,
an Hachette UK company.
www.hachette.co.uk

Contents

Great BEACHES, lovely **ISLANDS**
... and Gods who LOVE to **INTERFERE** in your **LIFE**

Welcome to Greece!

What do you know about ancient Greece?
Probably that it was full of thinkers called philosophers.
Or perhaps that it was the home of democracy. Or that
its warriors tricked the Trojans with a wooden horse.
Or that its myths are still popular today. Correct?

Well, none of that is WRONG,
but it's only PART of the story.
We're going to take you behind the scenes.

Hot facts

★ **Greece** is made up of a rugged peninsula and many islands in the Aegean Sea.

★ **Ancient Greece** was never a single country. It was a collection of city-states. They often co-operated but they also fought among themselves.

★ **The dominant** city-states were Athens and Sparta.

★ **Athens is famous** for being the first democracy in the world. It also produced many famous philosophers.

★ **Life in Sparta** was dominated by the army.

★ **Greeks settled widely**, and started colonies in countries including what are now Turkey, Sicily and Italy.

* ALL AT SEA! *
Having so many islands, it's no
wonder the Greeks are great seafarers.

RISE OF THE CITY-STATES

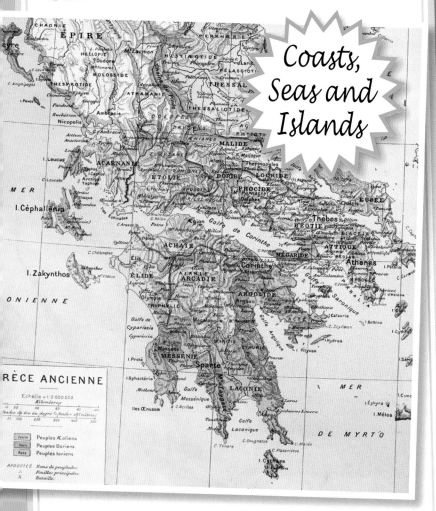

Coasts, Seas and Islands

- The roots of Greek civilisation began when the Minoans lived on Crete in around 3000 B.C.E.

- In around 1250 B.C.E. Greek warriors defeated Troy in Asia Minor. This victory became the basis for the famous myths of the Trojan Wars.

- Greece went through a 'dark age' between 1100 and 700 B.C.E.

- The first Olympic Games was held in honour of the god Apollo in 776 B.C.E.

- Athens began a golden age around 500 B.C.E. Many famous buildings were constructed in Athens, including the Parthenon.

- In 146 B.C.E., after a period of being ruled by the Macedonians, Ancient Greece became part of the Roman Empire.

It's a Classic!
Greek artists and sculptors influenced Western art for centuries. Their ideas were passed on first to the ancient Romans – and in the 14th century to the artists of the Renaissance.

A capital PLACE

Athens is the envy of the world. Not only is the city beautiful, it is also a centre of culture and learning. 'People power' rules here – we aren't the world's first democracy for nothing. If you've got a few hours in the city, there's plenty to see.

You can see the Acropolis from ANYWHERE in the city

The Parthenon
This huge temple is dedicated to the goddess Athena, our patron saint.

The High **Point**

Place of retreat
Acropolis means 'high place' – it was a place of safety if a city was under attack.

The Acropolis is the rocky high point of Athens – literally. Most Greek cities have an acropolis that can act as a citadel, or fortress. This outcrop dominates the whole of Athens. It was rebuilt by the ruler Pericles. Climb up and visit the huge temples – but be warned. If you visit when our assembly is meeting on Pnyx Hill – every 10 days – be prepared for a scrum. At least 6,000 men will be there to vote on new laws. You can tell who has turned up late: they are daubed with red paint. The men vote by each holding up one hand. It's well worth seeing.

On **Every Tourist's** list: The **temples** of the **ACROPOLIS!**  Theatre of **Dionysus**

Piraeus

We Athenians have always been seafarers. Our port is Piraeus, about 15 kilometres (9.3 miles) from the city. The navy is our main defence, so Piraeus stands between us and our enemies.

Mighty Athena
The statue is made of gold and ivory. It is 12 metres (36 feet) tall.

the Parthenon

If you look up from anywhere in Athens, you'll see the Parthenon, Athena's temple. If you didn't know how important Athena is to the Athenians, her temple would show you. The temple, dedicated to the goddess of wisdom, is the biggest and most beautiful building in our lovely city.

As well as the colours of the friezes around the top, notice the pillars outside. They look perfectly regular, don't they? It's a trick … they are narrower at the top. That's how the sculptors made them appear straight – otherwise the top would look thicker than the bottom when you looked up.

Don't **Lose** your **Marbles**

No, not toy marbles. The Parthenon marbles are carved friezes around the building. You'll see episodes from our history and scenes from myths and portraits of our gods. It's like a visual tour of Athenian culture and history.

Gorgeous **Gallery**

On the Acropolis, make sure to see the Erechtheion. It's another temple built by Pericles. The back porch is supported by six huge statues of women. These are the caryatids – and they're the Athenians' favourite pin-ups!

The **Tourist** *Trail*

You can find evidence of the Greeks everywhere around the Aegean Sea. These are some of our favourite places – they're mostly associated with our distant past.

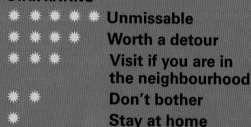

STAR RATING

✸ ✸ ✸ ✸ ✸ **Unmissable**

✸ ✸ ✸ ✸ **Worth a detour**

✸ ✸ ✸ **Visit if you are in the neighbourhood**

✸ ✸ **Don't bother**

✸ **Stay at home**

Palace for a BULL

Crete ✸ ✸ ✸ ✸ ✸

This lovely island is just 95 kilometres (60 miles) from the mainland. Its highlight is Knossos. Minos, king of the ancient Minoans, built this 1,300-room palace with running water and flushing toilets while the rest of Greece was living in caves. Check out the underground maze where the Minotaur – the half-man, half-bull monster – once lived. Just as well our hero Theseus killed him (read how he did it on page 21).

Troy ✸ ✸

Do you know the phrase 'Beware Greeks bearing gifts'? Well, the Trojans didn't. The Greeks left a hollow horse outside Troy in Turkey and pretended to leave.

The Trojans took the horse inside the city – with our soldiers hidden inside. When night came, they opened the gates and let the rest of the army in. Of course, because our soldiers then burned the city, there's not actually much to see!

Also worth a look: **Macedon:** Home of **Alexander** the **GREAT**, the Greek who conquered most of Asia.

Mycenae

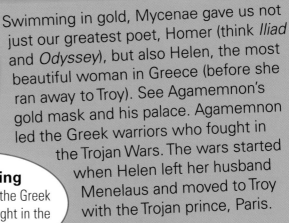

Swimming in gold, Mycenae gave us not just our greatest poet, Homer (think *Iliad* and *Odyssey*), but also Helen, the most beautiful woman in Greece (before she ran away to Troy). See Agamemnon's gold mask and his palace. Agamemnon led the Greek warriors who fought in the Trojan Wars. The wars started when Helen left her husband Menelaus and moved to Troy with the Trojan prince, Paris.

Heroic king
Agamemnon led the Greek warriors who fought in the Trojan Wars

Mount Olympus

The home of the gods is the tallest mountain we know: at 2,917 metres (9,570 feet). You can see Mount Olympus from miles away, even from the sea. You don't need us to warn you not to get too close to the top. No-one wants to disturb the gods. They wouldn't be amused!

Top of the world!
The gods who live on Olympus are known as the Olympian gods –obviously!

Delphi

If you want to know what the future holds, head for the temple of Apollo on Mount Parnassus. Ask your questions and Apollo will answer through the oracle's mouth. But don't rush him. Leave a day for your visit, so you can sacrifice a goat to the god.

One to **AVOID:** Sardis **(TURKEY):** Capital of Lydia – but **FAR** too close to the **Persian** Empire.

9

Welcome **to my** Beautiful *Home*

Is this your dream home?

Stuck for decorating ideas? Check out the latest designs in homes – and find the perfect place to live.

Men only
The men have their own room – it's called the andron and it's used for entertaining.

47 Agora Street
Athens AZ2 6812

A BUYER'S GUIDE

- Your house needs to keep the heat in during our cold winters, and stay cool during our hot summers. Look for small windows with wooden shutters.
- A courtyard in the middle of the house is a must, and will help to keep the rooms cool, so get the largest one you can. The altar to the gods should also be here.

- Make sure there is a room set aside for women, the gynaeceum, and the andron for the men.
- To be really fashionable, look out for a tub in the bathroom. But don't expect modern toilets. Everyone uses a bucket with a seat.

Home DECORATION: ✔ We **LOVE** the idea of a special COOL room to **STORE** food.

In a spin
Women use spindles to spin thread from wool.

Goddess
As you know from myths, even goddesses weave their own clothes.

Upright loom
Looms can be large – so keep them in their own rooms.

homeStylist

★ Men, inviting your friends round for a symposium (that's a banquet)? Make sure your andron has the padded couches that are all the rage. And no women – unless you count the female companions, hetairai.

★ Ladies, make sure your gynaeceum is comfortable because you'll spin and weave every day. But make sure you have time to chat if one of your girlfriends calls round.

★ We Greeks are known for our hospitality. Your mother probably told you to treat every guest in your home like a god – and she was right. The gods do like to check up on we humans, so offer every visitor the same hospitality you would offer Apollo!

Arts and Crafts

Weaving is a great skill for any woman. Even Athena, our goddess, wears a tunic she wove herself. Having a weaving room is vital. That way you can leave the loom in place. You won't just weave clothes, but also bedding, wall hangings and rugs.

Her Indoors

It can be pretty dull being a woman. Once you're bathed and dressed, what is there to do? There's always weaving, but who wants to spend all day in the gynaeceum? It would be great to head to the agora to catch up with the gossip – but respectable ladies just aren't seen out and about.

Talking point
Discuss your latest weaving with your friends!

Don't worry about the bedrooms. They're usually left virtually empty **APART** from a **bed** and a wooden **CHEST**.

Food and Drink!

We Greeks are a pretty healthy bunch. Mother Greece provides everything we need to eat well and keep our bodies in tip-top condition, from olives to grapes.

DO I EAT IT OR DRINK IT?

Kykeon is a mixture of wine (our favourite drink) and barley. It's nutritious and cheap. If you add enough barley you can make a kind of porridge. This makes a good evening meal, served with cheese, fish, fruit or vegetables.

Party Tips

Any self-respecting Athenian man likes to invite his friends to his home for a banquet or symposium. Here's how to be sure the evening goes well.

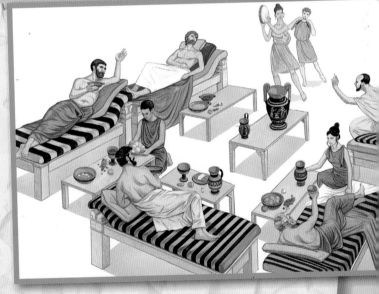

1 ★ The first part of the evening is for food. Provide the best food you can afford – meat if you can, otherwise fish, cheese and bread are fine.

2 ★ Once your guests have eaten enough, it is time to drink. But make sure you provide snacks like chestnuts or honey cakes to absorb the alcohol.

3 ★ Try and stay sober enough to talk to your guests, or play a table game.

4 ★ Try to stay awake and keep everyone else awake. Those couches can be very comfortable – but there's always music and dance to end the evening, so don't snooze through it!

Food for thought: ✔ Eat **FOUR** meals a day: **breakfast**, lunch, a light afternoon meal, then **DINNER**.

Spartan Soup

Those Spartans are known for being tough, so they don't waste time eating nice food. Spartan men eat black broth. It's a stew made from pork (most Greeks don't eat much meat), salt, vinegar … and animal blood. The idea is that it makes them stronger.

Honestly, I don't think the gods like wild boar.

Food for the Gods

Everyone wants to keep the gods happy. The best way is to offer them a sacrifice. It needs to be meat, but any kind will do. We give the gods meat because it's so special that we Greeks rarely eat it. It's saved for treats – if you can afford it! Only the Spartans make a point of eating pork.

Game animal
The Greeks hunted boar and other wild animals.

Gift from the gods

Sacred oil
Olive oil was so sacred it was used to bless kings.

Athena's Gift

The olive was Athena's greatest gift to Greece. Think of all the ways we use olives. You can eat them; you can crush them to make olive oil for cooking or for burning in your lamps. You can even use them to make cosmetics. The doctor Hippocrates uses olive oil to treat skin diseases. He makes tea from olive leaves and flowers to work magic on stomach ache and sore eyes.

Keeping up
Appearances

Greeks! We can't all be Helen of Troy but there's no reason not to look our best. It's what Aphrodite, the goddess of beauty, would expect from us.

I'm far more beautiful than Aphrodite!

Helen's face 'launched a thousand ships' – when the Greeks went to war

Helen's Make-up **Tips**

Helen of Troy is the most beautiful woman in the world. The Trojan War was fought over her. Here's how to get the look.

★ **Hair** – wear it long and curled. Blonde is everyone's favourite (use vinegar to bleach darker hair). Olive oil or wax will give hair that glossy Helen sheen.

★ **Skin** – the paler the better! Use lead to whiten your skin and keep out of the sun. Our olive skin loves the sun.

★ **Eyes** – accentuate your eyes with eyeshadow made by mixing charcoal and oil.

★ **Eyebrows** – the stronger the better. Use a dark pigment like charcoal to give your eyebrows definition. Monobrows are in right now!

★ **Lips** – keep them red. Mix red oxide with clay for a vibrant colour. Any of the mixture left over makes a stunning rouge for the cheeks.

Aphrodite, the goddess of beauty, is one tough lady. Aphrodite's jealousy of Helen, her half-sister, caused the Trojan War. She made Helen fall in love with the Trojan hero Paris. Helen's husband, the king of Sparta, headed to Troy with the Greeks to get her back. That was the start of the 10-year war – and the end of Troy.

Makeover magic: ✔ Ladies – Take **care** with your **HAIR!** Your SLAVES will help you **CURL** it.

Get your **chitons** on

This year's must-have is the chiton. Of course, it's every year's must-have. Everyone loves these floor-length robes because they're so simple to wear. Just drape a rectangle of cloth around your body and fasten it at the shoulder with a pin. Men's chitons are even simpler, as they only reach the knees.

If you can afford it, go for silk in a bright colour. On a more limited budget? Stick with wool or linen for hot summer days. Use a colorful pin to keep all that fabric in place, and cinch the waist with a belt.

Pin it up
A pin at the shoulder will hold the chiton together to avoid embarrassment.

Give it a belt
Give the chiton more shape by adding a belt around your waist.

Strappy sandals
There's only one choice of footwear.

Dear Achilles,

I need new shoes. You've got the most famous heel in history. Do you have any advice for me?

A Confused Walker, Corinth

Dear Confused,
Sandals are really the only choice (unless you go barefoot). For a journey, try the new kind with thick cork soles. They're good for stony ground. Make sure the ankle strap protects your Achilles tendon. Take it from me. It can be vulnerable – especially to a poison arrow!
Achilles

Men – still wearing a long **chiton**? **Get** with **IT!** It shouldn't come any **LOWER** than your **knees**.

15

Body *Beautiful*

Keeping in shape and looking good is the duty of every self-respecting Greek. The Olympic Games are a huge celebration of human strength. Athletes come from all over Greece.

Apollo became the model of the ideal male body

perfect Proportions

Famous sculptors like Phidias and Myron have worked out the perfect body proportions for men and women. Here are their tips.

★ The length of your neck should measure half the width of your shoulders.

★ Beautiful, slim-shaped ankles are a must for a woman. Think Aspasia, who has the perfect pins (she is the mistress of the ruler Pericles).

★ A man's height should be six times the length of his foot.

★ A woman's height should be eight times the length of her foot.

★ Your second toe should be as long as your first.

Workout with Apollo: ✔ Lift **KETTLEBELLS** to build arm muscles! ✔ Squats for the LEGS

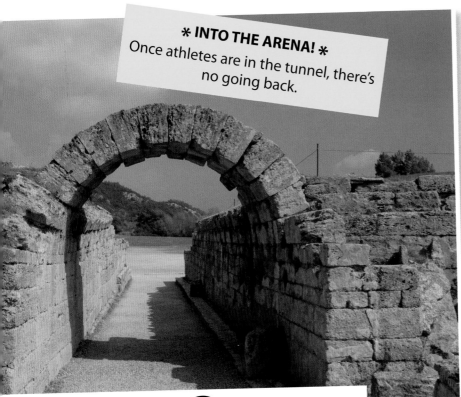

Olympic Games

The waiting is almost over. The Olympic Games are only a month away. It doesn't seem nearly four years since the last games, does it? A call has gone out to all male athletes from all city-states who want to take part.

Remember: no slaves or women can apply (though ladies compete in their own games in honour of Hera, queen of the gods).

★ **Day 1:** The *hoplitodromia*, a killer 190-metre (625 feet) sprint in full armour, is only for the very fittest of athletes.

★ **Day 2:** The pentathlon will really sort the men from the boys. It includes sprint, long jump, javelin, discus and wrestling.

★ **Days 3 and 4:** *Pankration* is a brutal combat sport in which any kind of attack is legal except biting or gouging out your opponent's eyes.

★ **Day 5:** The chariot races always have plenty of thrills and spills. Remember the time 40 chariots entered the race and only one finished? The others all crashed.

Meet A Sporting Hero

We caught up with top wrestler, Milo of Croton:

Q. Milo, you are competing in your seventh Olympics. Are you feeling confident?
A. Once you walk through that tunnel into the arena, it's important to believe in yourself. I've got six Olympic titles behind me. I hope to make it seven.

Q. Croton always produces fantastic athletes. Is it something in the water?
A. (laughs) Well, we Crotons make sure we are always in shape so that we can fight our enemies if need be.

Q. How will you deal with this new wrestler from Croton? They say he wrestles at arm's length.
A. With any luck, I can get in close to him and squeeze him in my trademark crush.

❌ Don't forget to **WARM UP**. ✔ Prepare for **WEIGHT** training with a 16-kilometre (10m-mile) **RUN!**

let me have
a *THINK*

If there's one thing Greeks are good at, it's thinking. Philosophy is Greek for 'love of knowledge' – and we have some of the best thinkers around. Here are some of the greatest.

I have a
Theory

Pythagoras is the go-to man for maths. He says that if a triangle has a right angle and you put a square on each of the three sides, the square on the longest side will have the same area as the other two combined – every single time. Try it for yourself.

TOP
thinkers
meet

Brain *Boxes!*

- Looking for a good school? Try Plato's Academy.
- Curriculum includes maths, music, philosophy, poetry and sports.
- Past pupils include Aristotle.
- Located just outside Athens.

Think it through
The philosophers like to take time to talk and debate their ideas.

Useful or not?:   Pythagoras's THEOREM is great for working out **areas!**

Five finkers!

Everyone should become vegetarian – but no-one should eat beans … because of wind!

Socrates (c469–399 B.C.E.)
The Father of Philosophy

Socrates started it all. He based everything on reason. He taught his pupils to argue point by point. Socrates never wrote anything down. It was his students who noted down his thoughts.

Plato (428–347 B.C.E.)
Arguing through Dialogues

Plato was one of Socrates' best pupils. He loved dialogue, when people with opposing views question each other to test their theories. Try Plato's Republic. It's a good read about humankind and society.

Epicurus (341–270 B.C.E.)
Father of Happiness

If you don't want to feel bad about feeling good, Epicurus is the thinker for you. He says people should only worry about having as much fun as they can.

Aristotle (384–322 B.C.E.)
Superbrain

Is there nothing that Aristotle can't do? Poetry, physics, metaphysics, history and logic are just some of his areas of expertise. No wonder Alexander the Great hired him as a teacher.

Diogenes (412–323 B.C.E.)
Life in a Barrel

Diogenes turned his back on wealth. He lives simply in a barrel. When Alexander the Great visited and asked if he needed anything, Diogenes asked him to move out of the way of the sunlight.

'Please move because you're blocking the sun.'
Diogenes

Plato's idea that the **UNIVERSE** is based on **MUSIC** sounds like **USELESS** hocus-pocus to us!

19

are **you** sitting *Comfortably?*

Who doesn't love a good story? Listening to the heroic deeds of the gods and heroes is always a blast. There are just so many great tales out there.

Epic **Poetry!**

You can read – obviously! – but most Greeks can't. But that doesn't mean they have to miss out on the best stories. Just be sure to catch up with the *rhapsode* when he comes to town. This travelling storyteller is easy to recognise from his cloak and staff. If he's any good, he will know many stories. Listen out for the set phrases he uses to describe things like the sea – they help him remember long poems.

Once upon a time there lived a beautiful princess named Helen…

That poem is EPIC!

Who's this Homer?

Homer is the poet who wrote our most famous epics. We all love these long poems about gods and heroes from ancient history. They are never written down, so they are passed on from generation to generation by memory. Homer's two most famous poems were the *Iliad* and the *Odyssey*. The *Iliad* described the Trojan Wars. The *Odyssey* was the story of Odysseus's journey home after the war.

That's **EPIC!:** ✔ Homer's not the **ONLY** epic **poet** in GREECE – don't forget **HESIOD.**

Mythic **WORLD**

There are **so many** myths about our gods and about the heroes who lived in the Golden Age of the past. **These are just a few of our favourites.**

Theseus and the **MINOTAUR**

In a labyrinth beneath King Minos' palace in Crete lived the minotaur: half-human, half-bull. The minotaur ate live children. It was Athens' turn every 12 years to send seven boys and seven girls as sacrifices. But Prince Theseus of Athens decided enough was enough. Helped by Adriane, the daughter of Minos, Theseus killed the minotaur and escaped from the maze by using a ball of thread Adriane gave him to help him retrace his steps.

King Midas

Greed Midas asked the god Dionysus for the power to turn things to gold. But even the king's children turned to gold when he touched them. Midas had to beg Dionysus to take away his power.

I love children!
(Especially when they're fried or baked in a pie.)

Orpheus in the **UNDERWORLD**

Orpheus was the best musician in Greece. When his wife, Eurydice, died, he went to the Underworld to try to bring her back. Hades, god of the Underworld, liked Orpheus's music so much that he agreed – as long as Orpheus didn't look at Eurydice until they were back above ground. But Orpheus could not resist a quick look – and Eurydice vanished. Orpheus was doomed to a sad life without her.

✖ Hesiod can be a **bit** of a **MISERY.** He says Greece's **GOLDEN AGE** was long ago – this is only the **age** of **IRON**!

21

Let's see a Show!

There's so much to do in Greece. We have the greatest playwrights in the world. If you don't fancy a play, there's always a festival to catch in Athens, Delphi or Epidaurus.

Know your plays!

You always know what to expect when you go to see a play. It's bound to be one of the three types:

● **Tragedy:** these plays always end badly for at least one of the main characters, usually to teach the audience a lesson.

● **Comedy:** No-one wants too much tragedy. Audiences also like a happy ending. Enter comedy.

● **Satire:** We would never, ever make fun of our gods – but our leaders are fair game. Politics makes a good subject for these cheeky criticisms.

IN THE AUDIENCE AT EPIDAURUS

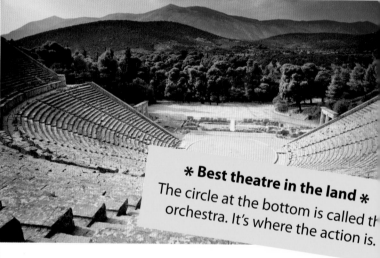

* Best theatre in the land *
The circle at the bottom is called the orchestra. It's where the action is.

The talented architect Polyclitus the Younger has come up with a winning design at Epidaurus. His new theatre there is cleverly built into a hill. The seats rise above the stage in a semicircle. That gives everyone a good view. The acoustics are great, too. You can hear the actors clearly, even from the very last row. And when the 14,000-strong crowd applaud at the end of the play, the noise is deafening.

At the **theatre:** ✓ Listen up! – our **ACOUSTICS** experts have made sure **everyone** can hear perfect

You'll laugh or cry!

a **theatre** trip

★ **Don't be a drama queen** – there aren't any. Only men are allowed to appear on stage.

★ **Don't expect expressive faces** – the actors all wear large, decorated masks so the people at the back can see.

★ **Don't lose the plot** – the chorus will explain what's going on. This group of actors comments on what's happening. They have to have good voices as they sing instead of speaking!

★ **Be united** – all plays follow the three unities. Unity of action: the play should have just one subject. Unity of place: the action should take place in the same place. Unity of time: the story (or drama) should take place over no more than 24 hours.

Chorus line
If you get confused about the story, they'll explain!

What's on

★ **Tragedy**

Aeschylus: the father of drama

Aeschylus has written a lot of plays about myth and history – more than 90, including *The Persians*, *Orestia* and *Prometheus Bound*.

Euripides: controversial figure

This writer of tragedies highlights the savage way Athens treats its defeated enemies. He's controversial, but audiences still flock to plays like *The Trojan Women* and *The Bacchae*.

Sophocles: Mr Rational

Sophocles writes tragedies about royal or noble families. They never end well. In plays like *Antigone*, Sophocles tried to show that people should rely on reason, not emotion.

★ **Comedy**

Aristophanes: Master satirist

If you like poking fun at our politicians – and who doesn't? – then Aristophanes' satires might be for you. Try *Wasps*, which pokes fun at the Athenian jury system (always a bundle of laughs).

✖ Don't forget a **CUSHION**: those **stone SEATS** get **UNCOMFORTABLE** after a couple of HOURS!

23

No Place for the Fainthearted!

Under protected
Warriors fight with swords and shields, but very little armour.

If you think life is too easy in Athens, think about a move to Sparta. That's where the tough guys live. They like life to be as hard as possible. That way, every Spartan is prepared for a fight at a moment's notice.

Who wants a FIGHT?

There is not much time for family life in Sparta. In fact, the Spartans don't think families are important at all. What matters more is that everyone is a member of the state of Sparta, not of their own family. By the age of seven, boys are packed off to military school. But that doesn't mean girls can stay at home – they get sent to school at the same age.

News just **in:** Spartan army joins other Greek states to **fight PERSIANS.** Victory at **Thermopyla**

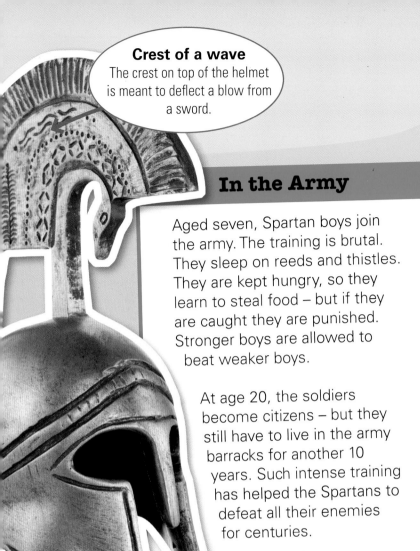

Crest of a wave
The crest on top of the helmet is meant to deflect a blow from a sword.

In the Army

Aged seven, Spartan boys join the army. The training is brutal. They sleep on reeds and thistles. They are kept hungry, so they learn to steal food – but if they are caught they are punished. Stronger boys are allowed to beat weaker boys.

At age 20, the soldiers become citizens – but they still have to live in the army barracks for another 10 years. Such intense training has helped the Spartans to defeat all their enemies for centuries.

Physical Fitness

Boys and girls are both super fit. But unlike the other Greeks, fitness in Sparta isn't about keeping the body beautiful. It's about being able to beat your enemy. Even weddings turn into physical battles. There are no honeymoons in Sparta. Instead, the couple fight until the man flings the woman over his shoulder and takes her home. Not very romantic!

It's hell for a Helot

Life is hard enough for a Spartan citizen, so imagine what it's like for a helot. These Spartans are not full citizens. They're barely better than slaves. On the plus side you can keep the food you grow that the Spartiate, or Spartan state, doesn't need. On the downside citizens can whip or even kill you without being punished. It all adds up to a pretty miserable life.

Bye-bye baby!

Being a cute baby isn't going to cut it in Sparta. Every baby is checked at birth. Those that seem too weak or sick to grow into useful citizens are condemned to a horrible death. They are thrown off cliffs or left to die from the cold on the side of the mountain. But a handful of sickly kids might be lucky enough to be raised as slaves.

I'd better get out of here!

Health and *Wellbeing*

Eating as well as we do and exercising regularly helps us to keep healthy. But we get ill from time to time when the gods want to punish us. That's why we're lucky to have such a modern medical service.

People leave Asclepius models of their body parts!

Snakes alive

The most famous of all Asclepius's sanctuaries is at Epidaurus. If you visit, don't be surprised to see snakes slithering around. They're everywhere, but don't worry. The snakes are sacred to Asclepius: that's why he's always shown with a snake twisted around his staff. (The snakes are not poisonous, by the way – that would be asking for trouble.)

A STAY IN HOSPITAL

- Your first port of call should be to pray to Asclepius. He is, after all, the god of healing, and you might be able to recover without any further treatment.
- If that doesn't work, spend the night in one of Asclepius' sanctuaries. You won't have to go far, because they are everywhere. While you sleep, Asclepius will appear to you in a dream and tell you what treatment is required.
- Next day, one of Asclepius' priests will administer the herbal remedies and show you exercises to do so that you get back to health.

Hippocrates' health tips: ✔ Keep **WOUNDS** clean. ✖ Avoid dog **BITES**; they can **cause INFECTION**

Medical **Miracle** Worker

If anyone invented medicine, it was Hippocrates back in the fifth century B.C.E. He took a scientific approach to finding out what caused sickness. Hippocrates used many herbal remedies to treat patients. Because he wrote everything down, we still have his observations. No wonder our young doctors today swear the Hippocratic Oath, which says they will do their best for their patients.

Doctor, doctor!
My arm hurts when I hold it like this.

The heart of things
Greek doctors believed intelligence was located in the heart.

Under the **Skin**

Have you ever wondered what's behind the perfect physique of Apollo or Helen of Troy? Well thanks to our clever doctors we are learning more about the inside of the body. The renowned physician Praxagoras has worked out that arteries carry blood away from the heart and veins carry it back. Soon, a doctor is bound to dissect a human body to find out what's inside!

Liver error
Praxagoras wrongly thought veins came from the liver.

Mystery fluid
Praxagoras said arteries carried a life force called pneuma, not blood.

A **Rational** approach

Hippocrates has shown that sickness has many causes. To keep healthy, try and keep your four humours – phlegm, black bile, yellow bile and blood – in balance. It's not always easy with our busy modern lives, but it is better to live in harmony with our bodies than to be ill!

Greeks *Abroad*

Potty about pots

Our skilled potters are in demand around the world. Every town has its own potters' quarter. With their exquisite shapes and detailed decorative painting, it's no wonder our pots are so popular.

Greeks get about. Some are traders. Others move abroad permanently. Take Magna Graecia – it is almost like being in Greece, except it's in southern Italy!

Talking Trade

When you are next at the agora, check out all the different products for sale. Quite a lot of it is imported, such as pepper, wheat and slaves from Egypt. In return, Greek traders export a lot of produce. We make far more olive oil and wine than we need, so we sell it overseas.

Phew, Pharos
A huge oil fire at the top of the tower guides ships to Alexandria harbour.

Wonder of the world

An Egyptian– Greek **Heroine**

Great news from Egypt! Queen Cleopatra is the latest in the Greek Ptolemaic dynasty to rule the country. Her capital is Alexandria, famous for its huge lighthouse. Cleo is now the most powerful woman in the world.

Also worth a **look:** Syracuse **(SICILY):** It's got loads of Greek buildings; **ARCHIMEDES** was born here.

A Buffer **State**

Homer taught us all about Asia Minor in Turkey (remember the *Iliad* and the *Odyssey*). Troy and Lydia are just two of the Greek outposts there. And, of course, this is our border with Persia, our greatest enemy. Having colonies in Asia Minor helps serve as a buffer to deter the Persians from attacking.

Mini Parthenon
Wherever we settle, we build the same temples we know from home.

Home Away **from Home**

Magna Grecia is a mini-Greece. Ever since our colonists started to arrive in southern Italy and Sicily in the eighth century B.C.E., we have been building cities and temples. Our colony looks as if it will last for centuries, despite this town of Rome that is becoming more powerful. We also have colonies in Cyrene (Libya), Emporion (Spain) and Antipolis (France).

Money Talks
Nowadays everyone uses coins to pay for goods. Bartering is very old-fashioned. The Athenian coins are probably the most sought after.

Make your point!
Triremes deliberately ram enemy ships with the spike at the front.

All at **Sea**

Much of Greece is islands, so sailing is the best way to get around. Merchant ships have large holds for cargo. A large eye on the side keeps away evil spirits. Merchant ships have sails. They are slower than our warships, the triremes, with their three banks of rowers and sharp spikes to hole enemy ships.

Steer **CLEAR:** ✖ **AL MINA** in Syria – it's **a COLONY** just for **trade**, so there's **NOTHING** to see.

Glossary

acropolis The highest part of a Greek city, which was often topped with a fortress, or citadel.

agora An open space used for markets or to hold meetings.

andron A room in a Greek house reserved for men.

city-state An independent part of Greece ruled by a city.

chiton A woollen tunic that came to the floor for women or the knees for men.

democracy A government system in which citizens vote to make decisions about government.

dynasty A series of rulers from the same family who pass on power to one another.

empire A group of countries that are ruled by a single ruler, the emperor or empress.

epic A long spoken poem that usually tells stories from history or myth.

gynaeceum A room in a Greek house reserved for women.

hetairai Female entertainers.

labyrinth A complicated network of passages like a maze.

loom A frame for weaving yarn to make cloth.

myth A traditional story that often involves gods or magic.

oracle Someone through whom a god or goddess speaks.

patron saint The god or goddess who protects a place.

peninsula A piece of land that is almost completely surrounded by water.

Persian Empire A powerful empire based in what is now Iran.

philosophy The study of the nature of knowledge and existence.

sanctuary A holy place or temple.

spindle A smooth rod used to twist and wind thread when spinning.

symposium A banquet for Greek men.

trireme A Greek or Roman warship with three banks of oars.

On the web

www.ancientgreece.co.uk/dailylife/
British Museum site about life in ancient Greece.

www.bbc.co.uk/schools/primaryhistory/ancient_greeks/
BBC Schools site dedicated to the ancient Greeks.

http://www.penn.museum/sites/greek_world/index.html
University of Pennsylvania Museum virtual gallery of the Greek world.

http://www.primaryhomeworkhelp.co.uk/Greece.html
Pages to help with homework assignments on Ancient Greece.

Books

Bingham, Jane. *Ancient Greeks* (Explore). Wayland, 2014.

Deary, Terry. *Groovy Greeks* (Horrible Histories). Scholastic Nonfiction, 2011.

Fowke, Bob. *Ancient Greeks* (What They Don't Tell You About). Wayland, 2013.

Green, Jen. *Ancient Greeks* (Hail). Wayland, 2013.

MacDonald, Fiona. *Ancient Greece* (100 Facts). Miles Kelly Publishing, 2009.

Napoli, Donna Jo. *Treasury of Greek Mythology: Classic Stories of Gods, Goddesses, Heroes and Monsters*. National Geographic Society, 2011.

Powell, Jillian. *Ancient Greeks* (Craft Box). Wayland, 2013.

Robinson, Tony. *Tony Robinson's Weird World of Wonders: Greeks*. Macmillan Children's Books, 2012.

Sims, Lesley. *Ancient Greece* (Visitors Guides). Usborne Publishing Ltd, 2009.

Index